Philo T. Farnsworth: The Life of Television's Forgotten Inventor

Russell Roberts

Mitchell Lane **PUBLISHERS**

PO Box 196 • Hockessin, Delaware 19707
www.mitchelllane.com

Unlocking the Secrets of Science

Profiling 20th Century Achievers in Science, Medicine, and Technology

Luis Alvarez and the Development of the Bubble Chamber
Marc Andreessen and the Development of the Web Browser
Oswald Avery and the Story of DNA
Frederick Banting and the Discovery of Insulin
Christiaan Barnard and the Story of the First Successful Heart Transplant
Tim Berners-Lee and the Development of the World Wide Web
Chester Carlson and the Development of Xerography
Wallace Carothers and the Story of DuPont Nylon
Francis Crick and James Watson: Pioneers in DNA Research
Jacques-Yves Cousteau: His Story Under the Sea
Raymond Damadian and the Development of the MRI
Gerhard Domagk and the Discovery of Sulfa
Paul Ehrlich and Modern Drug Development
Albert Einstein and the Theory of Relativity
Willem Einthoven and the Story of Electrocardiography
Philo T. Farnsworth: The Life of Television's Forgotten Inventor
Enrico Fermi and the Nuclear Reactor
Alexander Fleming and the Story of Penicillin
Henry Ford and the Assembly Line
Robert Goddard and the Liquid Rocket Engine
Otto Hahn and the Story of Nuclear Fission
William Hewlett: Pioneer of the Computer Age
Godfrey Hounsfield and the Invention of CAT Scans
Edwin Hubble and the Theory of the Expanding Universe
Robert Jarvik and the First Artificial Heart
Willem Kolff and the Invention of the Dialysis Machine
Barbara McClintock: Pioneering Geneticist
Lise Meitner and the Atomic Age
Joseph E. Murray and the Story of the First Human Kidney Transplant
Linus Pauling and the Chemical Bond
John R. Pierce: Pioneer in Satellite Communications
Charles Richter and the Story of the Richter Scale
Sally Ride: The Story of the First American Female in Space
Edward Roberts and the Story of the Personal Computer
Wilhelm Roentgen and the Discovery of X Rays
Jonas Salk and the Polio Vaccine
Edward Teller and the Development of the Hydrogen Bomb
Selman Waksman and the Discovery of Streptomycin
Robert A. Weinberg and the Search for the Cause of Cancer
Stephen Wozniak and the Story of Apple Computer

Philo T. Farnsworth: The Life of Television's Forgotten Inventor

Printing   2   3   4   5   6   7   8   9   10

Library of Congress Cataloging-in-Publication Data
Roberts, Russell, 1953-
   Philo T. Farnsworth: the life of television's forgotten inventor/ Russell Roberts.
      p. cm. — (Unlocking the secrets of science)
Summary: A biography of the persistent inventor whose interest in electricity led him
   to develop an electronic television system in the 1920s.
Includes bibliographical references and index.
   ISBN 1-58415-176-5
1. Farnsworth, Philo Taylor, 1906-1971—Juvenile literature. 2. Electric engineers —
   United States—Biography—Juvenile literature. 3 Inventors—United States—
   Biography—Juvenile literature. 4. Television—History—Juvenile literature. [1.
   Farnsworth, Rhilo Taylor, 1906-1971. 2. Inventors. 3. Television—History.] I. Title. II.
   Series.
TK6635.F3 R63 2002
621.388'0092—dc21   2002011055

ABOUT THE AUTHOR: Russell Roberts has written and published books on a variety of subjects, including *Ten Days to a Sharper Memory, Discover the Hidden New Jersey,* and *Stolen! A History of Base Stealing.* He also wrote *Pedro Menendez de Aviles* and *Bernardo de Galvez* for Mitchell Lane. He lives in Bordentown, New Jersey with his family and a remarkably lazy, yet fiesty calico cat named Rusti.

PHOTO CREDITS: cover: AP Photo; p. 6 Hulton/Archive; p. 9 Hulton/Archive; p. 10 AP Photo; p. 13 AP Photo; p. 16 University of Utah; p. 20 Corbis; p. 26 AP Photo; p. 31 AP Photo; p. 32 Hulton/Archive; p. 34 Corbis; p. 40 AP Photo.

PUBLISHER'S NOTE: In selecting those persons to be profiled in this series, we first attempted to identify the most notable accomplishments of the 20th century in science, medicine, and technology. When we were done, we noted a serious deficiency in the inclusion of women. For the greater part of the 20th century science, medicine, and technology were male-dominated fields. In many cases, the contributions of women went unrecognized. Women have tried for years to be included in these areas, and in many cases, women worked side by side with men who took credit for their ideas and discoveries. Even as we move forward into the 21st century, we find women still sadly underrepresented. It is not an oversight, therefore, that we profiled mostly male achievers. Information simply does not exist to include a fair selection of women.

   This story is based on the author's extensive research, which he believes to be accurate. Documentation of such research is contained on p.47.

   The Web sites referenced within were all active as of the publication date of this book. Given the fleeting nature of some internet sites, we cannot guarantee they will all be active when you are reading this book.

Contents

Chapter 1
A Day-Dreaming Farm Boy   7

Chapter 2
The Boy Who Loved Science   11

Chapter 3
Early Television   17

Chapter 4
Farnsworth's First Television Picture   21

Chapter 5
Competition!   27

Chapter 6
Legal Troubles   35

Chapter 7
A Sad Ending   41

Philo T. Farnsworth Chronology   45

Television Timeline   46

Further Reading   47

Works Consulted   47

Glossary of Terms   48

Index   48

Philo T. Farnsworth is shown here at 28 years old, with his wife, Elma (Pem). He is explaining the intricate details of the television apparatus that he had worked on since he was 14 years old.

Chapter 1

A Day-Dreaming Farm Boy

One day in the latter part of 1921, a 15-year-old farm boy was mowing a field of hay on a farm near Rigby, Idaho. But his mind wasn't on his work. Instead, he was thinking hard about something that would one day change the world: television.

The boy, who was named Philo Taylor Farnsworth, often used the time he spent working on his chores around the farm to think about possible solutions to scientific problems. But sometimes that could be dangerous.

Earlier that year, he had read about a contest sponsored by *Science and Invention* magazine. The editor wanted people to send in ideas for inventions that could prevent automobile theft. It did not matter that young Philo had only seen a few cars in his life. He knew that he could do it.

So one day he thought about how to stop car thieves while he was plowing a potato field with a team of horses. He was concentrating so much on his ideas that he absent-mindedly dropped one of the horses' reins onto the ground. This could have caused great injury to the boy. He might have tripped and stumbled onto the plow and cut himself very badly. It could have been even worse. Not long before, a careless farmer had fallen onto the sharp points of his plow and died.

Fortunately, his father had seen that his son was in danger. Walking carefully so as not to cause the horses to panic, he picked up the fallen reins. But when he gave the reins back to his son and told him to be more careful, Philo had simply shouted, "I've got it! I really think it will work!"

As it turned out, Philo did get it. He'd thought of an invention that worked on the principle of magnets. It was the most advanced invention anyone had come up with to stop car theft. So his "magnetized anti-theft ignition system" won the prize. With part of his winnings, Philo bought the first pair of long pants he ever owned. That meant he wouldn't have to wear short pants when he played his violin in a local dance band.

Now, on this afternoon when he was mowing hay, his busy mind was again wrestling with another scientific problem. He knew that radio electronically transmitted sound through the air. Why not use electricity to send pictures through the air as well?

Philo turned around to look at the hay he had just cut. The hay had fallen horizontally onto the ground in orderly rows. Each row lay neatly on top of another. Suddenly a thought struck the boy. Why couldn't he invent a device that would electronically "read," or scan, visual images by reading them horizontally—one row on top of another, just like the hay? Then it could transmit the electronic images at lightning speed through the air to another device. The second device would scan the images it had just received and turn them back into pictures for the human eye to see.

And so it was that a 15-year-old Idaho farm boy figured out how to make television by electricity possible. Little did Farnsworth know that he would spend much of his life trying to perfect electric television.

John Logie Baird was a Scottish engineer and another television pioneer. He gave a successful public display of his mechanical television in London in January 1926. Baird was investigating mechanical TV while Farnsworth was developing electronic TV.

A young Philo T. Farnsworth, probably at work on some television-related problem.

Chapter 2
The Boy Who Loved Science

You've probably heard people say that Willie Mays was born to be a baseball player, that Charlie Chaplin was born to be a movie comedian or that Michael Jordan was born to be a basketball player. Philo T. Farnsworth was born to be an inventor.

Farnsworth was born on August 19, 1906, on a farm in Beaver City, Utah. His parents were Lewis and Serena Farnsworth. He was named for his grandfather, who was a leader of one of the first groups of Mormons who settled in Utah. They made a long, hard overland trek from Illinois in covered wagons. Grandfather Philo had even built the log cabin in which his namesake was born.

His father was always looking for a better job or a better farm for his family to live on. So young Philo moved around a lot.

Even though his parents did not have much money or a fancy home, they were determined to give their son every opportunity to learn and educate himself. When Philo was three, his father took him to see a steam-powered railroad locomotive. The boy climbed into the cab and the engineer explained how it operated. When he came home, he drew a diagram of what he had just seen.

His favorite book as a small boy was an old Sears, Roebuck catalog. It was filled with pictures of exciting new products such as toy trains, alarm clocks and cameras. Seeing them excited his imagination. So did talking to his aunt one day on a telephone. There were so many wonderful things being invented. And many of them used electricity, which the Farnsworths didn't have.

When he was six, Philo declared that he was going to be an inventor when he grew up, like Thomas Edison or Alexander Graham Bell. Just like Edison, Philo wanted to spend his life conducting experiments in a laboratory. He would spend hours telling his parents about some new device that he wanted to invent, and the scientific principles upon which it was based. Patiently his mother and father listened to him. They also took him to the local library whenever possible and allowed him to read all the latest scientific magazines and textbooks. They did not want to ever discourage his imagination.

Sometimes Lewis Farnsworth helped his son with his science projects. Once they built a device that enabled Philo to trace the movement of the stars and planets.

When he was just eight years old, Philo became "the man of the family" when his father temporarily left home to clear land on an Indian reservation. He had three younger siblings and a fourth one was on the way. One of Philo's most important duties was taking care of Tippy, his very own pony.

But the Farnsworths moved again, this time to Vernal, Utah and Philo was forced to say goodbye to Tippy. On the new farm, Philo cared for a flock of lambs until they were old enough to sell. When he sold them, he bought a violin with his profits. He practiced long and hard on it, and became good enough to play in a local dance band. But as important as playing the violin was to him, science was even more important.

When Philo was around 11 years old, the family moved to Idaho. They had relatives there and the farmland was better. The Farnsworths didn't have a car and couldn't afford

Alexander Graham Bell, who invented the telephone, was one of Farnsworth's heroes.

to take a train. So just like their ancestors, they set out in three covered wagons. Philo drove one of them. The trip took about five weeks and covered nearly 500 miles.

In 1919, they moved a few miles to a farm near Rigby which belonged to Lewis's brother. When they arrived, Philo was in for a very pleasant surprise. The farm contained its own electrical generating system for lighting, heating water, and other uses. Farnsworth soon learned how the generator operated and kept it in good running order. He enjoyed working on it so much it was even suspected that he would deliberately break it from time to time just so he could fix it!

One chore that Philo hated was to hand-operate his mother's washing machine. He found an old electrical motor, fixed it up and hooked it to the washer. The motor operated the washer so that he didn't have to do it by hand any more.

Philo was encouraged by his success with the washing machine. He began taking apart anything mechanical that he found on the farm, trying to create more laborsaving devices. Any machine he encountered fell victim to his relentless curiosity.

"We never had an alarm clock that worked," his sister Agnes once said, referring to her brother's habit of taking everything apart.

But there was a hidden benefit to Philo's tinkering. At an age when many other boys were still learning how to read, write and do math, Philo already understood a great deal about science and why things work. He even was able to wire the local Mormon meeting house for electricity.

Once he attached a wire to a telephone pole and ran it to his friend's house. Then he attached another wire to another pole and ran it to his house. This enabled him and his friend to communicate by Morse Code. Of course, this knocked out everybody else's phone service, but no one was very surprised when Philo was found to be the cause. Everyone knew that he liked to experiment.

In the autumn of 1921 Philo entered Rigby High School. There he met a science teacher named Justin Tolman, a man who would greatly influence his life. Even though he was only a freshman, Philo asked if he could sit in on the senior chemistry class that Tolman taught. Tolman agreed, and soon Philo was asking questions that showed that his understanding of science and chemistry was extremely advanced. Tolman and his young pupil began coming in to school early and staying late to discuss science and work out the answers to questions that Farnsworth raised. In fact, the two spent so much extra time at school that the janitor complained!

But as much as Farnsworth asked questions about all aspects of science, he concentrated on one particular area. That was the problem of how to electronically transmit both audio (sound) and video (pictures) through the air. In other words, Philo Farnsworth was interested in television.

"Looking back," Tolman said later, "I realize that nearly every question he asked me had some bearing on the problems of television. I see now that it was all coming together in that head of his."

What Tolman did not know was that those discussions he had with Philo would have a major impact on the future development of television.

Philo was certain that electronic television was the way to make the best transmission and receiver possible. Here he is shown with the transmitting set of the apparatus he developed in the 1920s.

Chapter 3
Early Television

Television was not a new concept. Sending moving pictures through the air along with sound had been something that had been discussed and attempted for many years. Farnsworth read all the magazines and journals that published any articles on the concept of television.

Most research at this time focused on what was called "mechanical" television. Mechanical television used special scanning disks called Nipkow disks. They were named after Paul Nipkow, the engineer who invented them in 1884.

These disks would spin around very quickly. One side was perforated with many tiny holes. Each hole would go over a specific portion of a brightly-lit image to be transmitted. The light reflected from the image would pass into the disk and be changed into electricity. The electricity contained a special coded form of the image. Portions of the image that were brighter generated more electricity. Then the light was transferred to another spinning disk in the television receiver, which decoded the electrical signals and recreated the image. It was called mechanical television because it contained moving parts.

The problem with mechanical television was that the pictures were very blurry. The receiving disk could not spin fast enough to "reassemble" the scanned image quickly enough to fool the human eye into thinking that it was seeing a whole picture. Farnsworth thought that mechanical television could never operate fast enough to produce a clear picture. Besides that, anything mechanical was always subject to breaking down. To him, therefore, transmitting images electronically was the only solution.

As early as 1908, a British electrical engineer named A.A. Campbell Swinton had speculated that electronic television might be possible through the use of what he called "kathode (now usually spelled cathode) ray beams" controlled by electromagnets. But many people, including Campbell Swinton himself, thought that developing television would not prove financially feasible. Farnsworth saw things differently. "I was only thirteen when I began studying the problem [of how to produce television]," he later said. "It wasn't long before I realized that whoever solved it would make a fortune."

Farnsworth knew that a light-sensitive material released a stream of electrons whenever light struck its surface. Campbell Swinton's cathode rays did the opposite. They changed invisible electrons into light. By utilizing these two effects inside a special vacuum tube—a tube from which all the air is removed—Farnsworth reasoned, it would be possible to transmit moving visual images by the use of electricity. This was because there was nothing to interfere with the movement of the electrons inside the airless tube. Thus the electrons could be arranged to form different patterns.

Farnsworth envisioned developing a special light-sensitive vacuum tube. The tube would react to the light and dark areas of an image sent to it. The tube would change these light and dark areas to electrons. These electrons would then be sent to a receiver, which would turn them back into light and dark areas. If the electrons could be "reassembled" quickly enough by the receiver, they would appear as a complete image to the human eye.

One afternoon in late February 1922, when Farnsworth was still just 15 years old, Justin Tolman arrived in the classroom in which he and Philo had their after-school scientific discussions. To Tolman's surprise, Farnsworth had covered the blackboard with drawings and mathematical equations. Tolman asked his young student what it all meant. Though Farnsworth's answer was simple, it would change the course of human history. "It means television through the use of electricity," he replied.

Farnsworth went on to explain that, just like the hay he had cut that had fallen into orderly rows, his special vacuum tube would scan visual images in orderly rows, one line after another. These scanned images could then be sent to a receiving tube. This tube would reassemble the images in order, one row after another. He called the tube in which the image would be changed into electricity an "image dissector." He called the receiving tube that reassembled the image back into a picture the "cathode-ray" tube. These tubes operated much faster than any mechanical device. And there were no moving parts to break down.

Tolman studied the young man's work, but could find nothing wrong with his reasoning. He knew that Farnsworth had progressed so far in his understanding of science that he was now beyond Tolman's ability to assist him. In fact, Farnsworth's idea of electronically scanning visual images had put him beyond the abilities of almost everybody at that time. Electronic scanning was a brilliant, revolutionary idea. But Farnsworth knew that sooner or later, another scientist would get the same idea. It was only a matter of time. He needed to develop his concept before that happened. It was like he was in a race—a race of ideas.

It was a race that would consume his entire life.

This photo shows a picture of Joan Crawford as it appeared on the cathode tube after being televised in an adjoining room in the Franklin Institute by Farnsworth.

Chapter 4
Farnsworth's First Television Picture

Over the next several days, Tolman listened in quiet amazement as Farnsworth explained his electronic television theories. The sandy-haired, blue-eyed teenager gave the teacher an amazing lesson in science. Tolman realized that this was an idea that could someday revolutionize mass communication and entertainment. Farnsworth asked him how he should proceed. Tolman told him not to tell anybody else about it, and to keep studying.

However, that was easier said than done. In the autumn of 1922, the Farnsworth family left Rigby for Provo, Utah. Philo did not initially go with his family, but joined them one year later. Taking Tolman's advice to heart to keep studying, he took correspondence courses in radio and electronics. He attended Brigham Young High School. He also enrolled at Brigham Young University as a "special student." He worked as a janitor to help pay for his studies. He even found time to romance a local girl named Elma "Pem" Gardner. He didn't have to look very far to find her. She and her family lived in the other half of the duplex that the Farnsworths occupied.

But on January 28, 1924, his father died of pneumonia. Philo had to shoulder much of the financial burden for supporting his family. He was barely able to finish high school.

Philo enrolled in the U.S. Naval Academy at Annapolis, Maryland. He believed that he could continue his education and at the same time earn enough money to send home.

But it didn't work out that way. There was one big reason this proved to be a bad idea. Under the rules at that time, he would have had to turn over all his future inventions to the U.S. government, and Philo intended to keep control of all his ideas. At the school, some of the sailors taunted him by calling him "Fido." So, from that point on, he became "Phil."

He got an early release from the school on the grounds that he was needed back home to help support his mother.

The nagging feeling that somebody, somewhere, must be thinking along the same lines as he was with regard to electronic television haunted him. He desperately wanted to develop his idea. But he knew that no company would hire him and let him experiment with his concept of electronic television without a college education. Without money, he couldn't go to school or set up his own independent laboratory to continue his experiments. His dream of inventing electronic television seemed to be fading away.

However, things were not all bad for Farnsworth around this time. He proposed to Pem on Christmas Eve, 1925.

Then in the spring of 1926, now living in Salt Lake City, the 19-year-old Farnsworth took a job helping two professional fund-raisers named George Everson and Leslie Gorrell organize the local fund drive for Community Chest charities. Everson's car had broken down earlier, and when it was fixed and ready to be picked up, Farnsworth volunteered to do it.

However, when the car again broke down and nobody seemed able to repair it, Farnsworth not only diagnosed the problem but also told the mechanics how to fix it. As Everson wrote in his book *The Story of Television*, that was when he realized that Farnsworth was more than just a teenager working odd jobs.

"Farnsworth impressed me as knowing more about the car than the man who made it," he said.

One night, after working late at the fund-raising office, Everson and Gorrell asked Farnsworth if he intended to go to college.

"I can't afford it," Farnsworth said. "I've been trying to find a way to finance an invention of mine, but it's pretty tough."

When the men asked what the invention was, Farnsworth told them about his idea for electronic television. They were startled. They had no idea what the boy was talking about.

That quickly changed. Over the next few days, Farnsworth told Everson and Gorrell additional details. As he spoke about his hopes and dreams, the thin, usually quiet Farnsworth was transformed. His blue eyes shone with excitement. His deep understanding and knowledge of science and electronics became evident.

More and more impressed with Farnsworth, the two men became determined to help him develop this innovative idea. When Farnsworth estimated that about $5,000 would be enough money to help him produce a working electronic television system, Everson said: "I have about six thousand dollars in a special account in San Francisco. I've accumulated it with the idea that I'd take a long-shot chance on something, hoping to make a killing. This is about as wild a gamble as I can imagine. I'll put that up to work this thing out. If I win, it will be fine, but if we lose I won't squawk."

Farnsworth, Everson and Gorrell drew up a partnership agreement to develop the idea. Farnsworth decided to go to Los Angeles, California with Everson and Gorrell to set up a laboratory. Farnsworth gave the astonished Pem three days to get married.

On May 27, 1926, Farnsworth and Pem were married. He was 19 and she was 18. Later that night, Farnsworth told Pem: "There is another woman in my life, and her name is Television." Then he went off to plan the California trip, leaving his new bride alone on their wedding night.

Once in Los Angeles, Farnsworth set up his research laboratory in the apartment that he and Pem lived in. Soon the apartment was overflowing with activity. The dining room was filled with Farnsworth's tools and machinery, the closet contained a tube-building machine, and an electrical generator sat in the carport. Everson Gorrell and Pem did what they could to help out.

This was during Prohibition, when people were forbidden to drink alcohol. The neighbors became suspicious of all of the activity in the apartment. They thought that Farnsworth was building a still and illegally producing liquor. Once they even called the police.

Finally, in late August 1926, Farnsworth was ready to demonstrate his television system. His image dissector, or television camera, was ready. So was his cathode-ray tube, the television set. He had spent just about all of

Everson's $6,000, and the young inventor was anxious to show that the money hadn't been wasted. With Everson and Gorrell in attendance, Farnsworth sent electrical power surging into his new television system.

It promptly blew up.

Farnsworth had failed to account for the power surge that occurred each time he operated his electrical generator. So the electrical overload had caused the explosion. Instead of being discouraged, Everson and Gorrell raised more money from a group of bankers in San Francisco. Farnsworth and Pem moved there, set up another laboratory on Green Street, and continued their experiments. But his new backers had given him only one year. In spite of his hard work, he was rapidly approaching that deadline.

Finally, on September 7, 1927, with Pem and several other people on hand, Farnsworth electronically transmitted the image of a straight line on a glass slide to a tiny, four-inch receiver in another room of the laboratory. Then an assistant moved the slide. The image of the line on the screen moved as well.

Everybody in the laboratory stood still. They all realized that they were witnessing something incredible.

"That's it, folks," said Farnsworth, his voice shaking with emotion. "We've done it—there you have electronic television."

Herbert Hoover (lower right), then Secretary of Commerce, took part in the first public demonstration of inner-city television broadcasting in 1927. Mr. Hoover, speaking in Washington, was seen on television screens at Bell Telephone Labs in New York.

Chapter 5
Competition!

B ut even as Farnsworth and his friends jubilantly celebrated their successful transmission, others were also making progress with their own experiments with television.

On April 7, 1927, the U.S. Commerce Secretary, Herbert Hoover, participated in a demonstration by the American Telephone and Telegraph Company (AT&T) of their new mechanical television system. Of course, the picture transmitted by the AT&T television system, like all pictures produced by mechanical television, was grainy and blurry. Another problem with mechanical television was that it was complicated to operate. People were used to just flicking a switch to turn on their radios. So it was extremely unlikely that they would want such a complicated device in their homes. It seemed that the only way to produce a simple television set that turned on and off at the flick of a switch was to do so electronically.

Experiments like the AT&T transmission were going on all the time, and Farnsworth was worried that somebody with more money and more resources than he had would figure out that electronics, not mechanical methods, was the key to making television feasible.

In fact, there was another man who was thinking along the same lines as Farnsworth. His name was Vladimir Zworykin. He was a brilliant engineer who worked for a large company—the Radio Corporation of America (RCA). Born in Russia, he had fled to America after the Russian

Revolution of 1917, when the Bolsheviks (who later became the Communists) gained control of the Russian government.

While employed by the Westinghouse Electric Company in 1922, Zworykin invented an electronic scanning cathode ray tube he called an iconoscope. It had many similarities to Farnsworth's image dissector.

In January of 1929, Zworykin told RCA Executive Vice-President David Sarnoff of his desire to produce a television that worked easily and electronically. It would be small enough to fit in the living room of the typical American family. In addition, this television would be inexpensive to produce.

Sarnoff had long been a supporter of television. In 1922 he had written a memo in which he had foreseen the likelihood that Americans would want to be entertained by programs transmitted into their living rooms. He had called for the creation of a broadcast network that would produce this type of programming. This network became the National Broadcasting Company (NBC), a division of RCA.

At first, NBC was limited to producing strictly radio programs. But Sarnoff believed that television, and producing television programs, was the wave of the future. He knew that the size, complexity and cost of mechanical television sets made it unlikely the average American family would want to buy them. But as he listened to Zworykin describe electronic television, Sarnoff thought that it was a product that people would want to own. RCA could make a fortune by building it. He approved Zworykin's research budget. Now Farnsworth had a serious rival.

Meanwhile, in San Francisco, Farnsworth had been busy trying to move to the next level with his experiments.

In *The Story of Television*, Everson wrote about how Farnsworth swooped into the laboratory every morning bursting with new ideas.

"His entrance was like a fresh wind bringing an argosy of new ideas to be tried out by his assistants," Everson wrote. "It was the repeated method of trial and error with new and untried ideas over months and years that assured the slow but certain progress in the improvement in the television picture."

In contrast to the neat square shape that is the modern TV, Farnsworth's television would have been more at home in a mad scientist's laboratory. Everson wrote that "In one room [was] the dissector tube with its coils and amplifiers. The dissector tube was hooked up to some panels containing the scanning generators. Leads were fed into a black box containing the amplifier. A copper tube led out of the amplifier into the receiving room."

Farnsworth had already demonstrated that a horizontal image—a straight line—could be scanned and reassembled electronically. In early May 1928, he wanted to demonstrate that vertical scanning was possible too. He set a small triangle on a slide.

At first everything went well. The image of the triangle appeared on the receiving set. Suddenly it disappeared. It was replaced by a strange swirling image. Farnsworth was horrified. What had gone wrong?

He soon discovered that a worker had been smoking a cigarette. The swirling image on the screen was cigarette smoke. That meant that his system could televise objects in motion! That was even better than he had hoped for.

It seemed as though Farnsworth was on the right track with his ideas of how to produce television. However, the people who were financing Farnsworth's work were becoming impatient. They had already spent approximately $50,000, and they wanted a return on their investment. They wanted to sell the lab and Farnsworth's discoveries to a big company for a large profit, and get out of the television business.

Farnsworth knew that he was in danger of losing control of his invention if everything was sold. Trying to obtain favorable publicity and persuade his financial backers to hold on, Farnsworth held a press conference on September 1, 1928. Before then his work had been secret. But at the press conference he revealed the details to the world.

"S.F. Man's Invention to Revolutionize Television," screamed the next day's headlines. Soon the story was being reprinted in newspapers across the country. Despite some ups and downs, including a fire that destroyed the lab in the autumn of 1928 (fortunately it was insured, and rebuilt), Farnsworth continued with his work. He knew that the commercial possibilities of television were enormous, and that whoever could finally perfect television would become wealthy. Farnsworth desperately wanted that person to be him.

The press conference was the beginning of continuing news coverage about Farnsworth's work. As more and more people read about him and his experiments, distinguished visitors like Guglielmo Marconi (the inventor of radio) and Douglas Fairbanks (the movie actor) started dropping by Farnsworth's lab to receive a television demonstration.

But the publicity also worked against Farnsworth too. It enabled his competitors to easily learn what he was doing.

One of those competitors was Sarnoff, who became the president of RCA in early January, 1930. A few months later, he sent Zworykin, the Russian scientist who was working along many of the same lines as Farnsworth, to San Francisco to visit the Farnsworth laboratory.

The details of that visit have stirred a historical controversy that continues to this day. Was Zworykin just pretending to be curious about Farnsworth's experiments? Was he really sent there by Sarnoff to spy on Farnsworth because he represented a rival to Sarnoff and RCA?

Farnsworth had patents on several important parts of his electronic television, including the image dissector. That meant that if Sarnoff and RCA wanted to use his parts, they would have to pay him royalties. Was Zworykin's visit

Guglielmo Marconi (left), a physicist and co-inventor of the radio, dropped by Farnsworth's lab one day to see a television demonstration.

David Sarnoff, general manager of RCA, shown here in August 1926. Sarnoff was determined that RCA would be the inventor of television, and he refused to pay Farnsworth any royalties on his inventions. Farnsworth turned down Sarnoff's initial offers to buy him out.

just a way to steal Farnsworth's ideas, build his own parts, and avoid having RCA pay him royalties?

The answers to those questions will likely never be known. What is known is that Sarnoff was spending a lot of RCA's money on developing television. Like Farnsworth, Sarnoff could foresee the vast value that television would have in the future. He felt that television would someday become a fixture in the American home, replacing radio as the prime source of entertainment. Sarnoff wanted RCA to reap the financial benefits. Farnsworth, as a potential competitor who held several important television patents, was standing in the way.

"The Radio Corporation does not pay royalties, we collect them," Sarnoff said. Considering Sarnoff's philosophy, his reluctance to pay Farnsworth for his patents would be understandable. To underscore that point, in 1932 RCA absorbed another possible competitor, the Jenkins Television Corporation, and took control of all their important patents. RCA didn't have to worry about paying Jenkins any royalties. Now they owned them.

There was no doubt that Sarnoff was very interested in Farnsworth's work. He even visited Farnsworth's laboratory himself, in May 1931. He said that he thought that RCA would be able to avoid using any of Farnsworth's patents and thereby not have to pay him any royalties. But he still offered to buy out Farnsworth for $100,000.

The $100,000 figure was very high for that time. In addition, Farnsworth was always struggling financially and could have used the money. But if he had agreed to Sarnoff's offer, Farnsworth would have lost control of all his patents. His dreams of fame and fortune with television would have been gone forever.

Farnsworth's idols were inventors like Thomas Edison. That was how he pictured himself, as a solitary scientist working in a laboratory. He did not want to work for a big company.

So, not surprisingly, Farnsworth turned down Sarnoff's buy-out offer. Although Farnsworth did not know it at the time, his refusal would begin a difficult and costly legal war with RCA over electronic television.

It was a war that would seriously injure Farnsworth.

This is a closeup of the transmitting section of the television device that was perfected by Farnsworth. In the round aperture can be seen the end of the dissector tube, which was the "revolutionary" device that enabled TV to do away with the scanning disks of mechanical TV.

Chapter 6
Legal Troubles

By this time it was becoming obvious that television was going to be the "wave of the future" in entertainment.

Late in 1930, using a transmitter set up on top of his lab, Farnsworth sent moving images to another television set across town. Some people have called this the first transmission through the air of electronic television pictures.

The broadcast proved that Farnsworth and Sarnoff were both right. The future in entertainment clearly lay in television broadcasts. Companies such as Philco and Zenith were also conducting their own television research. Everybody wanted to be the one to perfect television.

So the stakes were very high indeed for the battle over who controlled television. It was a battle that Sarnoff did not intend for RCA to lose.

RCA was a large, multi-million dollar company, while Farnsworth had to watch every dollar he spent carefully. To try and make things more even between the two of them, Farnsworth signed a deal with the Philco Company in June 1931. At that time Philco was the largest manufacturer of radios in the United States. Under terms of the agreement, Philco would provide the money and equipment for Farnsworth's work. In return Philco would be able to freely use Farnsworth's patented television technology, which they hoped would allow them to compete with RCA.

The deal with Philco forced Farnsworth to move his work and his family from San Francisco to Philadelphia, where Philco had a television research laboratory. Late in

1931 Farnsworth began his own television broadcasts over a station called W3XE. The broadcasts were not like what we see on television today. They were short, in black-and-white, and consisted mainly of cartoons. The only places they could be received were where a Farnsworth television set had been placed. But it showed that Farnsworth was moving ahead.

Unfortunately, Farnsworth's biggest competitor—RCA, with Sarnoff and Zworykin—had their laboratories just across the Delaware River from Philadelphia, in Camden, New Jersey. They could receive the Farnsworth broadcasts. That let them keep an eye on Farnsworth's progress.

The pictures that Zworykin and RCA beamed out from Camden could also be received by Farnsworth, who nervously watched them. The pictures were very similar to his. With the resources of mighty RCA behind him, Zworykin could win the race to perfect electronic television.

In 1932, tragedy hit the Farnsworth family. On March 7, Farnsworth's year-old son Kenny suddenly died. Philco would not let Philo accompany Pem back to Utah to bury their son. The company said that his work was too important to let him leave. That incident played a part in Farnsworth's decision to leave Philco in the summer of 1933.

Now Farnsworth was again on his own, and struggling to compete against the giant resources of RCA. To help get publicity, he set up a television camera at the entrance of the Franklin Institute in Philadelphia beginning on August 24, 1934. People could see themselves on a small television receiver as they walked inside the museum. Today we are used to seeing ourselves on television when we walk by the electronics section in a department store, but in 1934 it was all very new and exciting. Hardly anybody had even heard of television, much less appeared on one!

Farnsworth also broadcast singers, musicians, and other entertainment from a small studio to an auditorium in the museum. People could watch everything on what was his largest screen so far. It measured 13 inches wide by 12 inches high.

But RCA kept pace. In 1935 they opened their own television studio in Rockefeller Center in New York. Soon they too were producing television programs.

Farnsworth had been pushing himself very hard and now all his hard work began to take its toll. In the early months of 1935, Pem saw a change in him.

"Feeling the hot breath of his well-funded competitors closing in on him, Phil continued to push himself unmercifully," Pem said. "He began to seek relief in a cocktail before dinner, frequently followed by one or two more during the evening before he could calm down enough to go to bed. This change in his routine began to cause me some real concern."

Farnsworth had other worries beside his television experiments. In May 1932, RCA had filed a lawsuit claiming that Farnsworth's television patents were too broad and covered too much about how electronic television worked. In addition, the company claimed that no teenage boy could have figured out the concept of electronic television, as Farnsworth claimed.

If RCA won the lawsuit, then Farnsworth's patents would be worthless. RCA would be free to use some of Farnsworth's inventions without having to pay any royalties to him. They claimed that their top television scientist, Alexander Zworykin with his iconoscope, had invented electrical television first.

For several years the two sides fought in court. Farnsworth even brought his old teacher Justin Tolman into court to help him. Tolman produced the notes and sketches of an electronic television camera tube that Farnsworth had made in his classroom years before to show that Farnsworth had thought of the idea first.

Eventually, in July 1935, Farnsworth won the case. His initial television patents were ruled valid. But RCA immediately appealed the verdict. Farnsworth and his small company had to face a depressing reality. With its vast financial resources, RCA could afford to keep fighting the patent battle for a long time. Farnsworth had scraped together the money to defend himself against RCA's legal challenges. It was money that he could have better spent on his work. He simply did not have the money that RCA had to keep fighting legal battles.

Worse yet, patents were only good for 17 years. After that, they ceased to be exclusive. Every year that passed without Farnsworth's receiving any royalty money from RCA was another year lost. Farnsworth suspected that part of RCA's plan was to keep him tied up in court so as to eat up as much of that 17-year period as possible.

Farnsworth was in a desperate situation. He and his workers at his television laboratory in Philadelphia sometimes barely had enough money to survive. As one of his assistants remembered: "To eat, we'd go to the Italian market in South Philadelphia and buy a gunny sack of week-old bread for one dollar. Bread, and rabbits that I raised on our farm, constituted my family's menu."

All of the strain and stress was destroying Farnsworth's health. He could not seem to relax and stop thinking about all his problems. Always thin, his weight began to drop, and he drank more.

Even deals to partner with AT&T and to operate his own radio and television manufacturing company—called the Farnsworth Television and Radio Corporation—did not help. RCA was getting the best of him and preparing to dominate the new television industry, and Farnsworth could not stop it.

At the 1939 World's Fair RCA put on a big television demonstration. Typically, World's Fairs are events at which futuristic inventions are introduced. This World's Fair introduced television to the American public. People began to get excited about this new invention, and to associate RCA with television.

The Farnsworth Corporation was nowhere to be seen. As George Everson explained, "we did not feel that we could afford to put in a television demonstration [at the World's Fair]."

It was Farnsworth's old problem again—lack of money. The World's Fair turned out very well for Sarnoff, Zworykin and RCA. They were talked and written about as the inventors of television. But television did not immediately become popular. The first sets were expensive. Few people rushed out to buy a television. Some people even said that television would never become popular.

Philo T. Farnsworth, however, had other problems.

Elma (Pem) Farnsworth is shown here in her Fort Wayne, Indiana home in January 1999 with memorabilia of her late husband, Philo T. Farnsworth.

Chapter 7
A Sad Ending

Throughout 1939, Farnsworth drank more and more, sliding deeper and deeper into depression. He felt that television, to which he had devoted practically his whole life, was slipping away from him. Farnsworth knew how bad his mental and physical health was becoming, but he was like a man on a rapidly spinning merry-go-round. He couldn't stop it from moving, nor did he dare jump off.

Events were quickly moving out of his control. At one point, he saw an RCA document that listed each of his patents and when they expired. He knew that if RCA just waited to begin mass producing television sets until his patents expired, he would not collect a single royalty check.

To add to his worries, World War II was looming in Europe. If the United States got involved in the war, American companies and factories would concentrate on products that would help in the war effort. Television production would cease until the war was over. That would mean even more years removed from the life of his patents.

World War II did indeed start in Europe on September 1, 1939. After Japan attacked Pearl Harbor on December 7, 1941, the United States entered the war. The government then banned the production of all consumer electronic products, including television, until the war was over.

All of these problems left Farnsworth feeling sick, tired, and depressed. Even though he was still a young man, stomach troubles had left him very thin. His face was filled with worry lines. He could not relax.

"Pem, I can't go on like this," he said to his wife at one point. "It's come to the point of choosing whether I want to be a drunk or go crazy."

When one doctor suggested that he might want to keep his fingers busy as a way of calming his nerves, Farnsworth took up another bad habit—smoking. Then he became addicted to a drug that he had been given to calm him down. The drug made him not want to eat and destroyed his frail health. He suffered a nervous breakdown. His weight dropped to a rail-thin 105 pounds. He was so sick he was hospitalized.

Eventually Farnsworth recovered enough to leave the hospital. He returned to a quiet home in Maine that he had purchased. But it would be a long struggle before he would get well. He suffered another setback when his brother died in a plane crash. Soon afterward, a fire destroyed Farnsworth's home.

Meanwhile, the emerging world of television continued without him. Sarnoff had become a wartime hero, attaining the rank of brigadier general. When World War II was over in 1945 he returned to RCA, where he had one priority: television. Soon RCA television sets were rolling off the assembly line, and an eager American public snapped them up. Beginning in autumn, 1947, Americans bought one million television sets within two years. RCA controlled eighty percent of the market.

The small Farnsworth Television and Radio Corporation could not compete with the gigantic RCA. On January 7, 1949, NBC broadcast a program celebrating television's birth. Sarnoff and Zworykin both appeared. Zworykin was introduced to the viewing audience as the "inventor of television." A few months later, the Farnsworth company was bought out by the International Telephone and Telegraph Company because of its continuing financial difficulties.

By then, another of Farnsworth's predictions came true. It turned out that there was big money in television. Over $100 million was spent early on by companies advertising their products on television. Sadly, Farnsworth himself did not benefit, either financially or emotionally, from television's success. Farnsworth blamed television for his troubles, and turned his back on it.

"For a while," Pem said, "he wouldn't even allow the word 'television' to be used in our home."

He was so unknown that when he appeared on the television quiz show "I've Got a Secret" in 1957, no one on the panel could guess who he was. But host Garry Moore paid tribute to him. "We'd all be out of work if it weren't for you," he said.

Farnsworth spent much of the remainder of his life working on a safe way to harness the energy generated by the fusion, or joining together, of atoms. He felt that nuclear fusion could someday light and heat homes, protect cities from destructive storms by "untwisting" tornadoes, and even provide the power for rocket flights to distant stars.

But just like with television, he had patent trouble with his nuclear fusion inventions. By now, Farnsworth was getting older, and he was tired of fighting. At one point, after he had given information to a patent attorney, he said: "I've given you all the material you need. Now I'm going to go home and get drunk."

He put aside his objections to watching television long enough to join millions of other viewers on July 20, 1969. U.S. astronaut Neil Armstrong became the first human to land on the moon. "Pem," Farnsworth said, "this has made it all worthwhile."

Philo T. Farnsworth died from pneumonia on March 11, 1971 at the age of 64. By that time, his name was just a ghostly echo heard among researchers when they talked about the early days of television. It appeared that the American public had forgotten him.

That wasn't entirely true. A large billboard on the outskirts of Rigby proclaims it as the home of "Philo T. Farnsworth, the inventor of television." The U.S. Postal Service released a special edition stamp to commemorate Farnsworth's life and ingenuity. In 1994, he was inducted into the National Inventor's Hall of Fame. Farnsworth Peak, named for him, is located in the Oquirrh Mountains that overlook Salt Lake City. It seems fitting that an antenna for broadcasting high-definition TV signals has been situated there because of its nearly 10,000-foot elevation.

Time magazine named Philo Farnsworth as one of the 100 most important people of the 20th Century, alongside such luminaries as Albert Einstein, Winston Churchill, Walt Disney and the Wright Brothers. Sarnoff also made the list. Zworykin didn't.

Perhaps Farnsworth's greatest honor came in 1990 when a statue proclaiming him as the "Father of Television" was dedicated in the United States Capitol in Washington, D.C. Today, visitors to the Capitol see a bronze figure of young Philo holding a vacuum tube and dreaming of television—just as he did so many years ago, when the world was so full of possibilities.

Philo T. Farnsworth Chronology

1906	born on August 19 in Beaver City, Utah
1912	declares intention to become inventor
1920	moves with family to Rigby, Idaho
1921	conceives of his image-dissector tube
1922	explains concept of electronic television to Justin Tolman
1923	joins family in Provo, Utah
1924	father dies
1926	signs partnership agreement with George Everson and Leslie Gorrell to develop electronic television; marries Pem Gardner
1927	electronically transmits straight line
1928	successfully demonstrates vertical scanning electronically; holds press conference to announce his results
1929	birth of first child, Philo T. Farnsworth III
1931	birth of second child, Kenny Farnsworth; signs deal with Philco
1932	young son Kenny dies
1934	sets up television camera at Franklin Institute
1935	wins patent interference case against RCA; birth of third child, Russell Farnsworth
1937	establishes Farnsworth Television and Radio Corporation
1939	decides not to display his television system at World's Fair because of lack of money
1948	birth of fourth child, Kent Farnsworth
1949	Farnsworth Television and Radio Corporation is bought out by International Telephone and Telegraph Company
1957	appears on "I've Got a Secret"
1950-60s	works on developing safe, inexpensive nuclear power
1971	dies of pneumonia on March 11

Television Timeline

1873	Scottish scientist James Maxwell shows relationship between electricity and magnetic fields
1884	German engineer Paul Nipkow invents the Nipkow disk
1887	German physicist Heinrich Hertz projects magnetic field in the air
1897	German scientist Karl Braun invents cathode ray tube oscilloscope
1908	A.A. Campbell Swinton speculates that "kathode ray beams" might make electronic television possible
1922	Russian engineer Vladimir Zworykin invents kinescope, a cathode-ray tube
1925	John Logie Baird and Charles Jenkins demonstrate mechanical television
1927	AT&T hosts mechanical television demonstration; Farnsworth successfully transmits straight line electronically
1929	Zworykin decides to pursue electronic television for RCA
1934	Communications Act of 1934 begins government regulation of television airwaves and establishes Federal Communications Commission (FCC) to enforce it
1939	RCA introduces television to the public at the World's Fair
1941	U.S. government suspends television production /World War II
1945	RCA introduces image orthicon camera tube designed by Zworykin that improves picture quality by higher sensitivity to light and dark
1947	war over, Americans enthusiastically begin buying television sets
1950	American Broadcasting Company (ABC) airs first Saturday morning children's programs
1951	first color television program is broadcast
1962	launching of communications satellite Telstar I enables live transmission of events from anywhere in the world
1967	Public Broadcasting System (PBS) is formed as alternative to commercial television
1976	Video Home System (VHS) and Betamax video recording cassette (VCR) systems are introduced in U.S.
1978	videodisc players are introduced
1980	introduction of portable video camera and recorders (camcorders)
1989	first broadcast of high definition television (HDTV) in Japan
1995	flat screen plasma televisions are introduced
1997	introduction of DVDs (Digital Versatile Discs)
2003	RCA previews a new 50-inch rear-projection HDTV based on Texas Instruments' Digital Light Processing™ technology

Further Reading

For Young Adults

Kent, Zachary. *The Story of Television.* Chicago: Children's Press Inc., 1990.

McPherson, Stephanie Sammartino. *TV's Forgotten Hero: The Story of Philo Farnsworth.* Minneapolis, MN: Carolrhoda Books, Inc., 1996.

Works Consulted

Everson, George. *The Story of Television: The Life of Philo T. Farnsworth.* New York: W.W. Norton, 1949.

Farnsworth, Elma G. *Distant Vision: Romance and Discovery on an Invisible Frontier.* Farnsworth Archives.

Fisher, David E. and Marshall Jon Fisher. *Tube: The Invention of Television.* New York: Harvest Books, 1997.

Godfrey, Donald G. and Christopher H. Sterling. *Philo T. Farnsworth: The Father of Television.* Provo: University of Utah, 2001.

Schatzkin, Paul. *The Boy Who Invented TeleVision.* TeamCom Books, 2002.

Schwartz, Evan T. *The Last Lone Inventor.* New York: HarperCollins, 2002.

Stashower, Daniel. *The Boy Genius and the Mogul: The Untold Story of Television.* New York: Broadway Books, 2002.

On the Internet

Philo T. Farnsworth Archives maintained by son, Kent
http://philotfarnsworth.com

San Francisco Chronicle Article 1928
http://www.inventorsmuseum.com/farnsworth.htm

Photos of Farnsworth
www.lib.utah.edu/spc/photo/p437/p437.html

History of TV
www.tvhistory.tv/Philo.htm

All about Philo T. Farnsworth
www.farnovision.com

Glossary of Terms

argosy an opulent (rich) supply

Communist political party advocating the principles of communism, especially as developed by Karl Marx and Vladimir Lenin

meeting house building used for religious worship

Mormon member of the Church of Jesus Christ of Latter-day Saints

patent government grant to an inventor for a stated period of time, conferring the exclusive right to make use of and sell an invention

Prohibition the legal prohibiting of the manufacture and sale of alcoholic beverages

royalties payments made to the holder of a patent for the right to use his/her invention

still a distilling apparatus used to make alcoholic beverages

Index

AT&T 27, 39

Bell, Alexander Graham 12

Bringham Young High School 21

Bringham Young University 21

Edison, Thomas 12, 33

Everson, George 22, 23, 24, 25, 29, 39

Farnsworth Television and Radio Corporation 39, 42

Fairbanks, Douglas 30

Franklin Institute 36

Gardner, Elma "Pem" 21, 22, 24, 25

Gorrell, Leslie 22, 23, 24, 25

Green Street 25

Hoover, Herbert 27

Marconi, Guglielmo 30

Moore, Garry 43

Mormons 11, 14

National Inventor's Hall of Fame 45

Nipkow disks 17

Nipkow, Paul 17

Philco 35-36

Prohibition 24

Rockefeller Center 37

Sarnoff, David 28, 31, 32, 33, 35, 36, 39, 42, 44

Swinton, A.A. Campbell 18

Tolman, Justin 15, 19, 21, 38

U.S. Naval Academy 21

Washington, D.C. 44

World War II 41, 42

World's Fair, 1939 39

Zworykin, Vladimir 27, 28, 31, 36, 38, 39, 42, 44